Planet Earth

Daniel Gilpin

KINGFISHER

NEW YORK

KINGFISHER
LONDON & NEW YORK

Copyright © Kingfisher 2011
Published in the United States by Kingfisher,
175 Fifth Ave., New York, NY 10010
Kingfisher is an imprint of
Macmillan Children's Books, London.
All rights reserved.

Distributed in the U.S. by Macmillan,
175 Fifth Ave., New York, NY 10010

Library of Congress Cataloging-in-Publication data
has been applied for.

Illustrations by Peter Bull Art Studio

ISBN 978-0-7534-6591-2

Kingfisher books are available for special promotions
and premiums. For details contact: Special Markets
Department, Macmillan, 175 Fifth Ave.,
New York, NY 10010.

For more information, please visit
www.kingfisherbooks.com

Printed in China
1 3 5 7 9 8 6 4 2
1TR/0411/WKT/UNTD/140MA

Contents

More to explore

On some of the pages in this book, you will find colored buttons with symbols on them. There are four different colors, and each belongs to a different topic. Choose a topic, follow its colored buttons through the book, and you'll make some interesting discoveries of your own.

For example, on page 6 you'll find an orange button, like this, next to the picture of Earth. The orange buttons are about forms of life.

Page 22

Life

There is a page number in the button. Turn to that page (page 22) to find an orange button next to another example of life on Earth. Follow all the steps through the book, and at the end of your journey you'll find out how the steps are linked and discover even more information about this topic.

Science

Environment

People

The other topics in this book are science, environment, and people. Follow the steps and see what you can discover!

Our planet, our home

What do people mean when they talk about our planet? Well, they mean the huge ball of rock and other material that we all live on. Our planet—Earth—is the only one we know of that is home to living things.

Water covers two-thirds of Earth's surface. Most of this water is salty water, held in the oceans.

Boats allow people to cross the oceans.

Earth, like all planets, is shaped like a ball.

....This is the Atlantic Ocean, which borders North and South America.

Earth has been photographed by satellites in space. This photo shows blue oceans, green land, and yellow-brown mountains. From space, all clouds look white.

Earth, seen from space

Weather happens in the air that surrounds Earth.

The highest point of a mountain is called the peak, or summit. •••••

Lightning may strike in stormy weather. •••••••

Low valleys lie between mountains.

Land is where Earth's surface sticks out above the oceans. Land can be flat, hilly, or mountainous. Most land is covered with soil and has grass or other plants growing on it.

butterflies

African elephants

People live in different countries in different parts of the world. Earth is home to more than six billion people.

Elephants are the biggest land animals. •••••

Animals, plants, fungi, bacteria, and all sorts of other living things share our planet. Some live on land, and others live in the oceans.

What is this?

① Earth

② stars in the Milky Way galaxy

③ Sun

Page 22

Earth in space

Earth is one of billions of objects in space. Our planet circles the Sun, and the Moon circles our planet. The Sun is actually a star, one of millions in our galaxy. Our galaxy is called the Milky Way. There are many millions of galaxies in space.

③

⑥

Earth moves around the Sun in an oval-shaped path called an orbit. There are seven other planets orbiting our Sun, too. Scientists use satellites like the one below to help them investigate the wonders of space. They take photographs and gather other information. Scientists are still looking for signs of life on other planets.

④

⑤

Page 27

This photograph shows pits, called craters, on the surface of the Moon.

Earth, Sun, and Moon

The Sun and Moon affect many things that happen on Earth. For example, the Sun gives us light and warmth, which most living things need in order to survive. The Moon affects the oceans, causing tides.

Sun

Here it is nighttime.

Earth spins on a tilt.

Earth spins around and around as it orbits the Sun. It takes 24 hours, or one day, to complete each full turn. Parts of Earth facing the Sun receive daylight. In parts that are facing away, it is night.

Here it is daytime.

Plants have leaves to help catch sunlight.

Sunlight is very important for life on Earth. Plants need sunlight to grow, and they provide us and many animals with food. The Sun also warms our planet. It drives the wind, rain, and other types of weather, too.

Children pick vegetables in Hawaii.

Sunrise lights up the sky.

Cold winter weather can bring snow and ice.

The Sun rises in the morning, when our part of Earth is moving into daylight. It sets as we move into night. The Sun is far away in space, but we can see it in the sky because it is so huge. The Sun is 109 times wider than Earth!

Seasons happen because Earth orbits the Sun once every year. When it is summer, our part of Earth is tilted toward the Sun during daytime, so we receive more of its heat and light. In the winter, we get less sunlight as our part of Earth tilts slightly away.

Like Earth, the Moon is lit by the Sun.

Earth's shadow often covers part of the Moon, so it looks like a crescent.

In an eclipse, the Moon blocks out the Sun.

Tides move up and down the beach.

A solar eclipse occurs when the Moon passes between Earth and the Sun. The Moon is much smaller than the Sun, but it looks the same size because it is closer to us.

Tides in the ocean are caused by the Moon. As the Moon moves around Earth, it pulls the water on Earth's surface toward it. Twice every day, the ocean moves away from the shore and back in again.

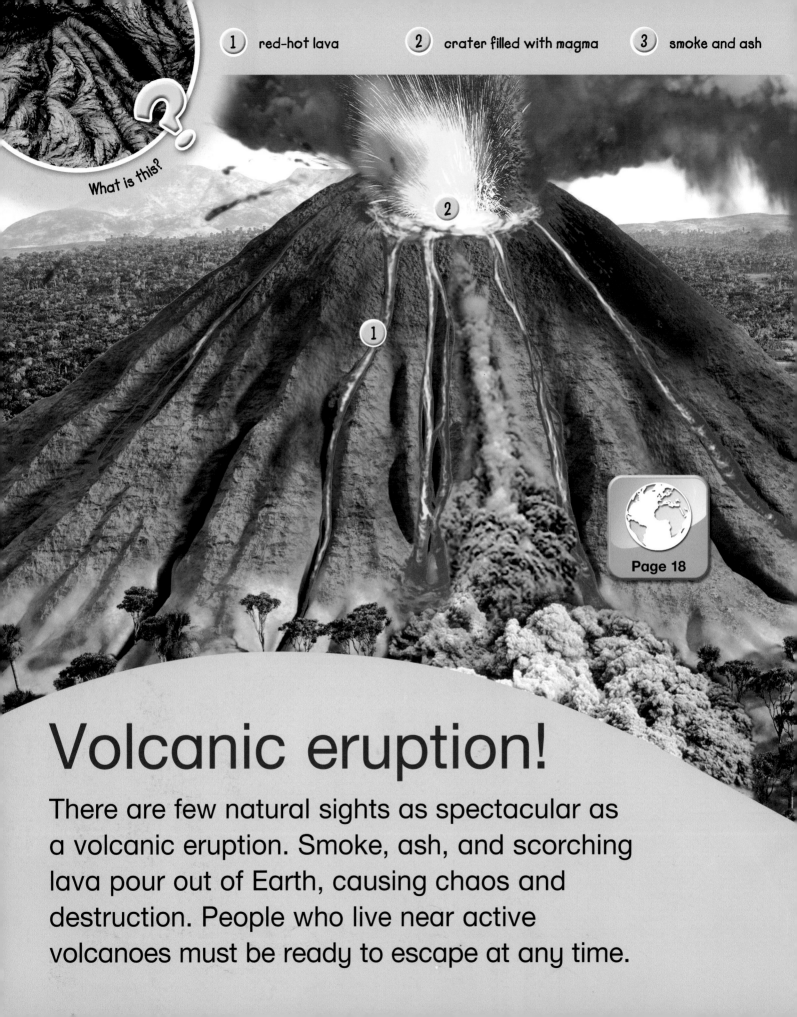

Page 18

Volcanic eruption!

There are few natural sights as spectacular as a volcanic eruption. Smoke, ash, and scorching lava pour out of Earth, causing chaos and destruction. People who live near active volcanoes must be ready to escape at any time.

③

The people of this farming village are being evacuated to safety as rivers of red-hot lava pour toward their homes. When a volcano erupts, lava can burn down houses. Ash fills the air and covers buildings and land. Eruptions can go on for days, weeks, or even years. Their effects often spread for many miles around.

Page 19

⑤

④

Page 15

⑥

↻ This is a close-up view of lava with a cooled, hardened crust on top.

Inside Earth

Earth is made up of different layers. On the outside is the crust, where we live. Inside it is much hotter, sometimes so hot that the rocks are liquid. The sizzling center of Earth is called the core.

Earth's crust is between 3 and 30 mi. (5 and 50km) thick. It is made up of sections called plates, which float on the mantle beneath.

The temperature of lava ranges from 1,300 to 2,400°F (700 to 1,300°C).

Land and oceans lie on Earth's crust.

outer core

inner core

lower mantle

upper mantle

Liquid rock inside Earth is called magma.

Lava is liquid rock that has burst through Earth's crust, usually from a volcano. When lava cools, it hardens and becomes solid. The rock it forms is called igneous rock. There are two other main types of rocks: sedimentary and metamorphic.

A volcanologist studies lava from a volcano.

An earthquake takes place when two plates in Earth's crust jerk suddenly against each other. This causes the ground to shake.

Earthquakes happen along fault lines like this, where two plates meet.

This is the San Andreas fault in California.

Valuable stones and metals are hidden in Earth's crust. In some places, people dig holes, called mines, to find them.

Gold is a precious metal found in some rocks.

This crown is made of gold and jewels.

The jewels are stones dug up from Earth's crust.

Fossil fuels, such as oil and coal, also come from Earth's crust. They lie in sedimentary rocks—rocks made from mud, sand, or other sediments that were buried in the past.

An oil rig drills for oil in rock under the ocean.

Mountain adventure

Earth has areas of land and ocean, and land has many forms. Mountains are huge, steep-sided rock masses that rise up from Earth's crust. They are found where plates in the crust have crashed together, pushing up giant folds of rock. The tops of mountains are the highest places on our planet.

Page 30

What is this?

1. Loose snow falls in an avalanche.

2. valley made by a glacier, or river of ice

3. distant mountain peaks

This is a magnified snowflake. All snowflakes have six points, and every snowflake is slightly different.

4

Page 23

6

These climbers are on a slope in the Himalayas—the highest mountain range on Earth. Up here, it is cold and windy and the air is thin, making it difficult to breathe. Mountaineers take special equipment and clothing to help them survive.

5

Page 19

4 Mountain peaks are often above cloud level.

5 Climbers use maps and satellite devices to find their way.

6 Oxygen tanks and masks help climbers breathe.

On the map

Maps are pictures that mark places on Earth's surface. On world maps like this one, we can see both land and oceans. Maps can give us a lot of information, including how high the land is and where different countries and cities are found.

Continents are the main landmasse on Earth. Below, the seven continents are shown in different colo

Islands are areas of land that are surrounded by water. The photograph below shows an island in French Polynesia.

On a map, French Polynesia is here. It lies in the Pacific Ocean.

NORTH AMERICA

SOUTH AMERICA

N

W   E

S

A compass rose shows us directions: north, south, east, and west.

Alps

Mountain ranges are drawn as symbols on this map. The tallest is the Himalayas in Asia. This skier is in the Alps, a mountain range in Europe.

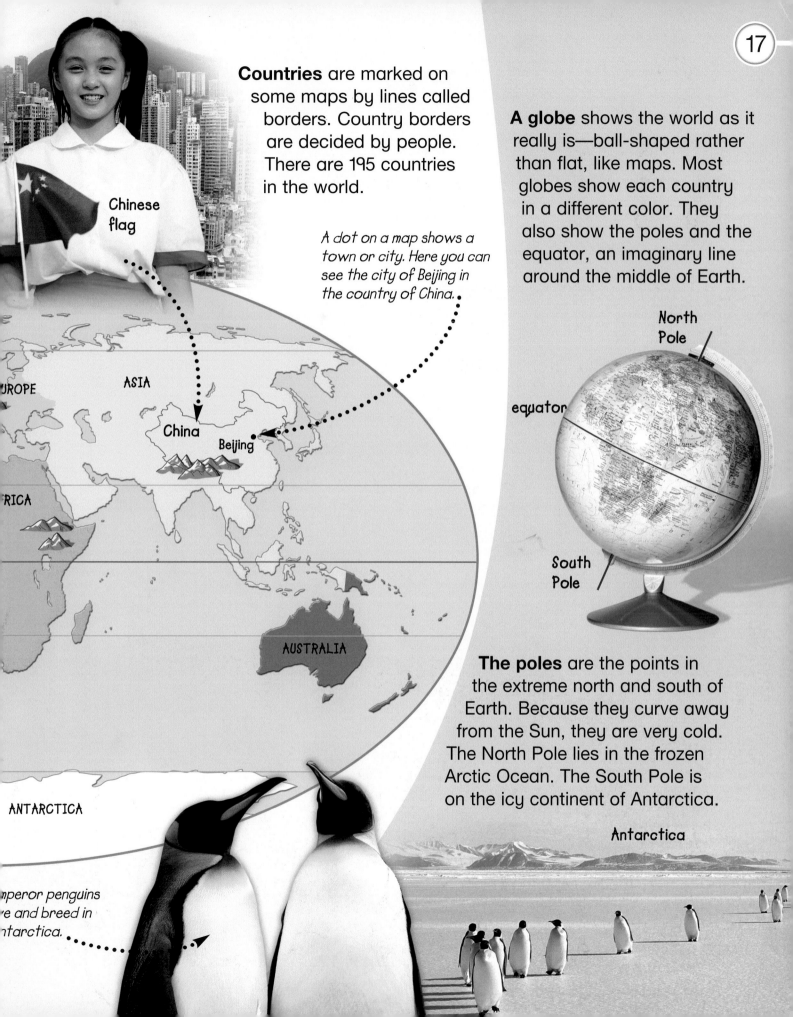

Countries are marked on some maps by lines called borders. Country borders are decided by people. There are 195 countries in the world.

Chinese flag

A dot on a map shows a town or city. Here you can see the city of Beijing in the country of China.

A globe shows the world as it really is—ball-shaped rather than flat, like maps. Most globes show each country in a different color. They also show the poles and the equator, an imaginary line around the middle of Earth.

EUROPE

ASIA

China

Beijing

AFRICA

AUSTRALIA

North Pole

equator

South Pole

The poles are the points in the extreme north and south of Earth. Because they curve away from the Sun, they are very cold. The North Pole lies in the frozen Arctic Ocean. The South Pole is on the icy continent of Antarctica.

Antarctica

ANTARCTICA

Emperor penguins live and breed in Antarctica.

Page 23

① seabirds on a cliff　② harbor　③ cave　④ cliff

What is this?

At sea

Most of the water on Earth is held in the oceans and seas. The area where land meets the ocean is called the coast. Oceans are powerful, with moving tides and crashing waves. They slowly wear down the land, forming natural arches, cliffs, and caves.

Page 30

5

6

The coast is a lively place. Many animals make their homes here, and many people like to live near the ocean. Some people, such as fishermen, do their jobs out on the water. In this picture, a fishing boat is bringing its catch back to harbor as the Sun rises in the morning.

Page 26

8

7

This is a close-up view of grains of sand. Sand is rock broken down by waves.

Watery planet

Water can be found all over our planet. As well as in oceans and seas, there is water in lakes, rivers, and ponds. Ice is frozen water, and it covers large areas of land. Some water falls as rain, and some is underground.

Water vapor rises.

Water evaporates.

Rivers flow into the ocea

Salty seawater fills the world's oceans. The three biggest oceans are the Atlantic Ocean, the Indian Ocean, and the Pacific Ocean. The Pacific Ocean is the biggest of all.

Rivers are full of fresh water and flow across the land.

The Seine River runs through Paris, France.

People fish on Lake Victoria.

Lakes are large areas of water surrounded by land. Most lakes are full of fresh water. Lake Victoria in Africa is one of the biggest lakes in the world.

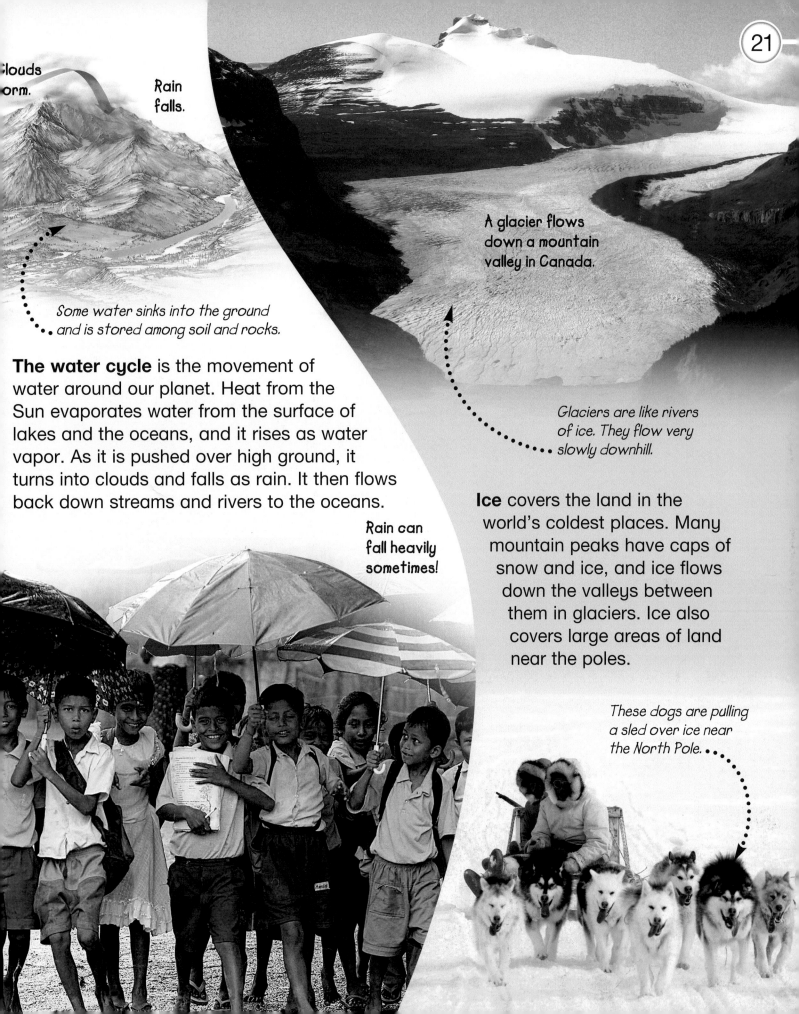

Clouds form.

Rain falls.

Some water sinks into the ground and is stored among soil and rocks.

A glacier flows down a mountain valley in Canada.

The water cycle is the movement of water around our planet. Heat from the Sun evaporates water from the surface of lakes and the oceans, and it rises as water vapor. As it is pushed over high ground, it turns into clouds and falls as rain. It then flows back down streams and rivers to the oceans.

Glaciers are like rivers of ice. They flow very slowly downhill.

Rain can fall heavily sometimes!

Ice covers the land in the world's coldest places. Many mountain peaks have caps of snow and ice, and ice flows down the valleys between them in glaciers. Ice also covers large areas of land near the poles.

These dogs are pulling a sled over ice near the North Pole.

Exploring the rainforest

Tropical rainforests are full of life. They are home
to thousands of different kinds of plants and animals.
Rainforest trees are some of the tallest on Earth.
The biggest are more than 200 ft. (60m) high.
Their branches are thickest at the top, forming
what is known as the canopy.

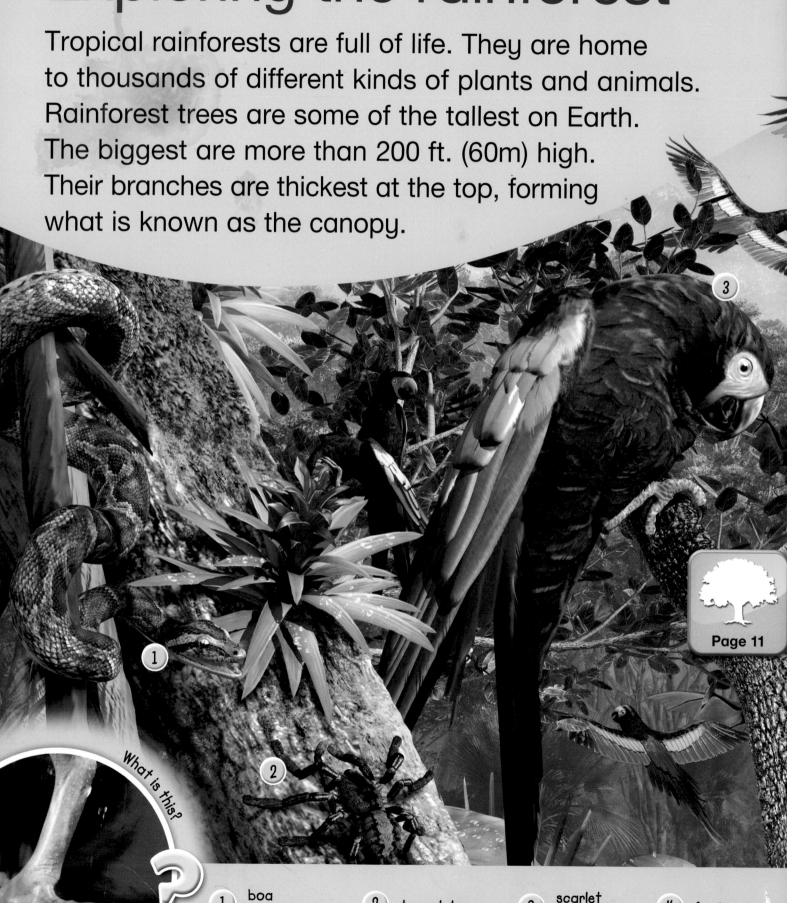

What is this?

Page 11

1 boa constrictor   2 tarantula   3 scarlet macaw   4 fruit bat

This is a tree frog's foot. Tree frogs have sticky pads on their toes to help them grip branches.

Page 14

At the end of the day, a group of scarlet macaws flies in to roost in a rainforest tree. Scarlet macaws are a type of parrot, and they live in South America. All around them, other animals and birds fill the treetops. Some eat leaves or fruit, but others—like the boa constrictor—are hunters that eat other animals.

Page 30

5   three-toed sloth   6   spider monkey   7   toucan   8   tree frog

Different biomes

A biome is a type of natural habitat—a place where particular kinds of plants and animals live. Tropical rainforest is a well-known biome, but there are many others, too.

Deserts are very dry places where it is tough for life to survive. Even so, deserts have their own plants and animals. Snakes and lizards are particularly common there.

Giraffes roam on savanna lands.

This thorny devil can go for a long time without water.

Temperate grassland is found in cooler countries, outside the tropics. In many places, it has been turned into farmland, and it is now one of Earth's rarest biomes.

Prairie dogs live on temperate grassland in the United States.

Bushes grow among the dry grass.

Savanna is the name given to open grassland in Africa and other hot parts of the world. It is home to herds of grazing animals and the creatures that feed on them.

A brown bear claws a forest pine tree.

Coniferous forest is made up of trees such as pine and fir, which have needles instead of large leaves. It covers large areas of Canada, Scandinavia, and Russia.

Most conifers have tall, straight trunks and downward-pointing branches.

Tundra is the biome closest to the poles. This is tundra in the summer.

Tundra plants are small and low growing.

Oceans and seas are home to more living things than any of the biomes on land. They are also the least explored parts of our planet. Less than 10 percent of the ocean floor has been fully mapped, and most of the ocean is too deep for human divers to survive.

Coral reefs are found in shallow tropical waters.

yellow angelfish

Using the land

Imagine the world without any people. It would look very different! People have changed the landscapes of Earth in many different ways. We have cut down trees, dug mines in the ground, made fields for farms, and built homes and roads. Every day, we change our planet a little more.

Page 30

What is this?

1 A plow digs up the soil.

2 logs from a planted forest

3 rock quarry

This is water flowing from a hydroelectric dam. Water turns turbines in the dam to make electricity.

This farmer is plowing a field for crops to be planted. Crops and farm animals, such as the cows in this valley, provide most of the food we eat. In the background, we can see logging in a forest and diggers in a quarry. The wood and stone from these will be used for building.

Page 15

4 town in the distance

5 hydroelectric dam

6 A reservoir stores water.

7 Wind turbines make electricity.

Earth and us

Every one of us has an impact on our planet. The homes we live in and the roads and railroads we travel on have changed the natural landscape. People have removed forests and other habitats to create building space as well as farmland for our food.

Villages and towns are small built-up areas of houses and other buildings. Cities are larger and cover greater areas of land. Some of the biggest cities are home to millions of people.

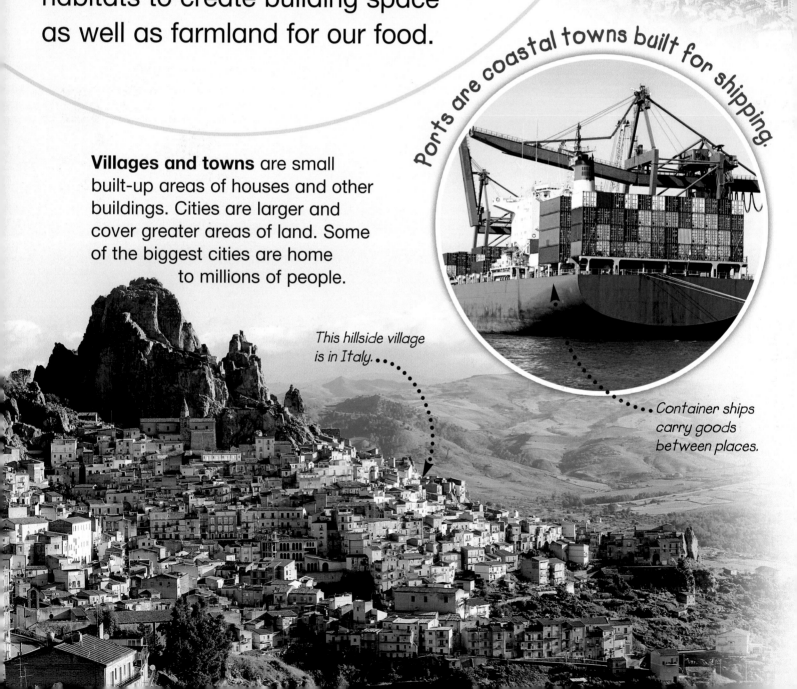

Ports are coastal towns built for shipping.

This hillside village is in Italy.

Container ships carry goods between places.

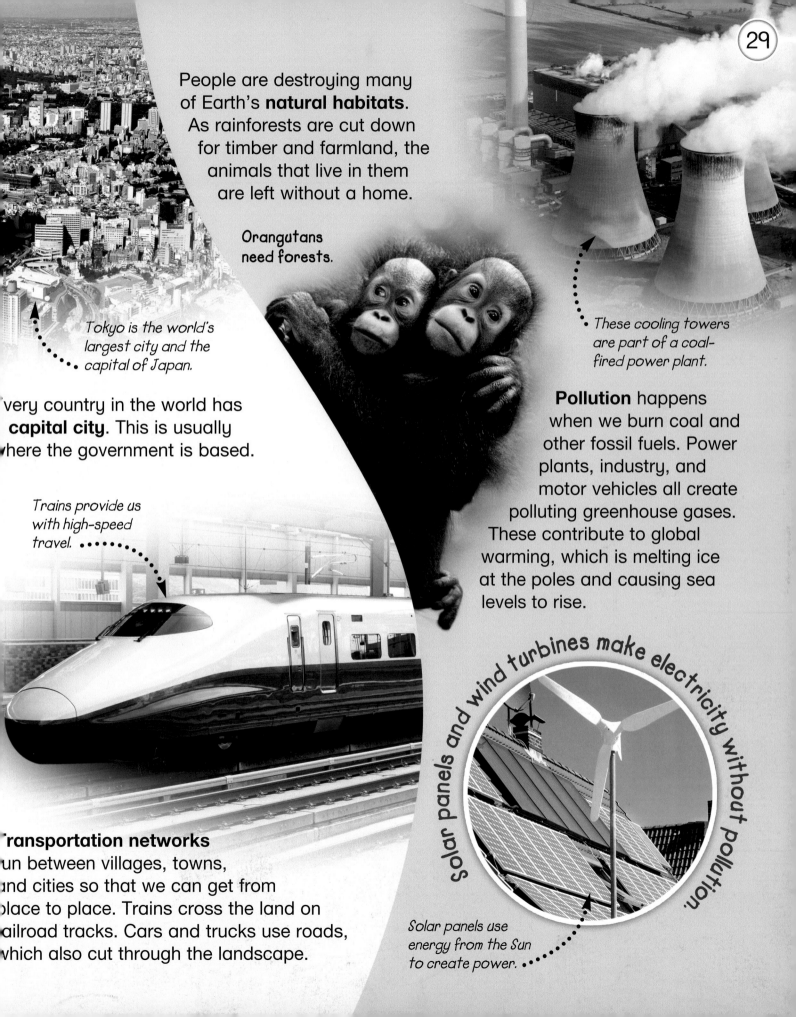

People are destroying many of Earth's **natural habitats**. As rainforests are cut down for timber and farmland, the animals that live in them are left without a home.

Orangutans need forests.

Tokyo is the world's largest city and the capital of Japan.

very country in the world has **capital city**. This is usually here the government is based.

Trains provide us with high-speed travel.

These cooling towers are part of a coal-fired power plant.

Pollution happens when we burn coal and other fossil fuels. Power plants, industry, and motor vehicles all create polluting greenhouse gases. These contribute to global warming, which is melting ice at the poles and causing sea levels to rise.

ransportation networks
un between villages, towns, nd cities so that we can get from lace to place. Trains cross the land on ailroad tracks. Cars and trucks use roads, which also cut through the landscape.

Solar panels and wind turbines make electricity without pollution.

Solar panels use energy from the Sun to create power.

flamingos, zebras, and a wildebeest

Life

Earth is the only place in the universe where we know life exists. Earth is home to millions of different **species** (types of living things). The animals above are species from East Africa.

Rainforests are home to thousands of different living things. They all have their own place and way of life. Bats and many other creatures are **nocturnal** (active at night), and others are active in the daytime.

Science

This **satellite** is helping map the Moon's surface. Other satellites are sent into orbit around Earth. They are used for everything from sending TV signals to forecasting the weather.

Building **dams** across rivers creates artificial lakes called reservoirs. These provide our towns and cities with water. Turbines in the dams produce electricity.

Environment

Volcanic eruptions completely change the landscape. Ash covers the ground and can crush or bury houses. Lava burns whatever it touches and then cools to form solid rock.

Cliffs look solid, but pieces often break off as waves pound them. This process is called **erosion**, and it can change the shape of a coastline over time.

arch

People

Java (in Indonesia) is the most densely populated island in the world, and it is dotted with volcanoes. Many of its 130 million people are farmers, growing rice in the rich volcanic soil.

The first people to climb the world's tallest mountain, **Everest**, were Sir Edmund Hillary and Tenzing Norgay in 1953. The youngest person to climb it was 15-year-old Ming Kipa in 2003.

Hillary and Norgay

More to explore

Volcanic ash forms rich soil that is perfect for growing crops. All plants need minerals and other natural nutrients in order to grow. Soil near volcanoes is particularly rich in these minerals.

Coastal cliffs and islands may look bare and lifeless, but they provide nesting places for all kinds of **seabirds**. There, they are safe from ground-living hunters such as foxes, which might otherwise eat the chicks or eggs.

seagulls

As altitude (height above sea level) increases, the amount of **oxygen** in the air goes down. Most climbers wear breathing equipment in high mountains to make sure they have enough oxygen.

Rainforest plants have given us many different **medicines**. One reason for protecting rainforests is to safeguard their plants so that scientists can continue to study them.

Rainforests are important to the **environment** because they help balance gases in the air. Plants take in carbon dioxide, a gas that can be harmful if there is too much of it. They give off oxygen, which all animals need to breathe.

rainforest plant

In **high mountain ranges**, temperatures are very cold. The water there is frozen. Glaciers are frozen rivers that change the landscape very slowly over time. The heavy ice grinds away at the ground and forms a U-shaped valley.

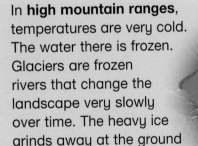

Fishing is an important industry for many coastal towns and villages. The people who work on fishing boats often work through the night, and they may be away for days at a time.

Most **farmers** do particular jobs at certain times of the year. Plowing takes place in the fall or early spring, depending on the type of crop to be planted.

Index